The Tao of Relationships

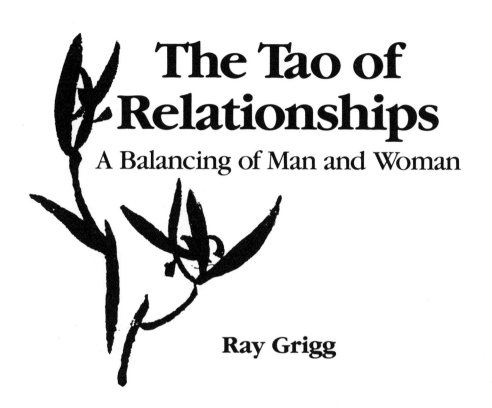

The Tao of
Relationships

A Balancing of Man and Woman

Ray Grigg

HUMANICS NEW AGE
Atlanta, Georgia

HUMANICS LIMITED
P.O. BOX 7447
Atlanta, Georgia 30309

First Edition

Many illustrations are from *The Mustard Seed Garden Manual of Painting,*
translated from the Chinese and edited by Mai-mai Sze, Bollingen Series,
Princeton University Press, New York, 1956. These illustrations, originally
reproduced by wood block printing, were created in the seventeenth century
by three brothers: Wang Kei, Wang Shih, and Wang Nieh.

PRINTED IN THE UNITED STATES OF AMERICA

Library of Congress Cataloging-in-Publication Data

Grigg, Ray, 1938–
          The Tao of Relationships.

                    1. Taoism.   2. Men.   3. Women   4. Courtship.
I. Title.
BL1920.G73   1987   299'.514178357   87-22643
ISBN 0-89334-104-5

To Joyce

Did the many arise from one urge?
Was it from the primordial mud
That came the first desire?

Where was the beginning?
How long has it been?

Is it in each one who seeks Twoness
And in each two who seek Oneness?

Can we choose not to love?

The Titles of the Chapters

INTRODUCTION

This book is about love but love is never mentioned or defined. Why? Because words are only metaphor. The experience they create is vicarious. Words obstruct understanding by creating the illusion of understanding; they confine and limit with the deception that the mystery has been captured. Words only represent the authentic. When there is naming, the name is mistaken for what has been named. Sages have always known this. They understand names. And lovers are sages.

Lovers live love. They are in it like rain is in raining and smiles are in smiling. But they cannot explain what it is because they are it. The Tao, like love, cannot be explained because we are it. But the "it" of the Tao and the "it" of love are not things. There are no things. What we call things are processes. There are no nouns even though we pretend there are. There is no love but there is loving.

The loving that is between lovers is between everything. It is between stone and stone, mist and mountain, grass and moon. Lovers call it love. Sages call it the Tao. Because of it rivers flow down valleys, green sprouts from seed to death, male and female unite and separate. It is called the Tao but it is not what it is called. It is everywhere but nothing knows what it is because it is what everything is.

The general urge that is everywhere is like the particular urge that is between each thing. The urge between man and woman for each other is the same urge that is between root and flower, leaf and soil, breath and wind. Man and woman come together like air and mist, rain and river, mountain and valley. They are part of the profoundly common. Each particular urge fulfills the general urge; each thing fulfills everything else. Knowing this moves each thing in particular and everything in general from the ordinary to the honoured.

To honour is to place ourselves within and to give ourselves over to the moving whole. We become one with the Tao. Only from within can there be control. But lovers, like sages, know they are not in control. Herein lies the paradox; loving means losing to find; it means being powerless by being within power.

The word "power" is not used in the Western sense but in the Taoist sense. In Lao Tzu's *Tao Te Ching* written in fifth century B.C. China, the word *te* (pronounced "der" as in "under") literally means virtue/power. It means to come into accord with the way the universe works (the *Tao*) and thus to have a selfless sense of power that comes not from opposing things but by flowing with them. The flowing with is the virtue; the being with is the power. This book is about balancing male and female virtue and power in order to find male/female virtue/power.

In the West, the common experience we have that is closest to virtue/power, is the energy between man and woman. Although that energy is warped and adulterated by sexual politics, it is nonetheless present as a primal force that confirms the charged condition between man and woman. In the Taoist paradigm, the polar interaction of yang and yin creates the dance that is the Tao.

Lovers feel the dance of that energy as being both profoundly right (virtuous) and profoundly moving (powerful). In the West, the lover's art is the most common way, perhaps the only way, that the sage's art is accessible to everyone. There is potential benefit in the West's sexual obsessiveness. But scientific materialism and mass media and commercialization, attributes that define a large part of our culture, do not contribute toward the sensitive wisdom that is needed to be the sagely lover.

Neither has the aesthetic, intuitive and empathetic nature of the sagely lover been assisted by the technological trappings in which we have dressed ourselves. The gap between who we are and who we think we are is considerable. We try with objective and empirical attitude to separate ourselves from everything, yet we are unable to detach ourselves from ourselves. We are subject that we cannot objectify. We are grounded by sexuality. Thus loving, with all its subjectivity, is made even more alluring by our efforts to be objective. Loving is the promise of ourselves to ourselves that we must keep. But it has become a bewildering spiritual quest because of the marketing of sex as commodity. Lovers cannot be objects to each other. A package cannot enwrap a mystery.

We live in a superficiality induced by our own ingenuity. We are stuffed with sensations and starved for feelings.

We know we are being sold chic shadows, that we cannot sell ourselves to ourselves. And we also know that just beneath our sexy shoes is thin ice. The style requires that we walk gingerly. When we deprive our sexual selves of our whole selves, sex is never enough. But just beneath the wrap that is designed for glitter and sales is a deep and haunting mystery. We know or remember or feel that if we jumped we would plunge deeply.

Beneath the marketing of sex and the manoeuvres of sexual politics, even ironically affirmed by them, is the irrefutability and inescapability of the fundamental omnipresence of our sexuality. We are sexual.

It is captivating and emancipating to know that sex is a part of ourselves that we can neither avoid nor contain. Is it in us or are we in it? Are we the servants of our own fulfillment? If the cliche and double-entendre will be forgiven, perhaps the tail does indeed wag the dog. It is auspicious that we cannot contain our sexual selves, that we are the masters who can only be masters by submitting ourselves to ourselves.

Acknowledging the suchness of things and living harmoniously within its nature is virtue/power. The first chapter of this book is called "The Tao" and the last chapter is called "Union." Sexual union is a physical enactment of the virtue/power, the *te*, of Taoism. It is the resolution of the physical dichotomy of male and female, of self and not-self. Man enters woman while woman receives man. Two bodies become one body. Physical separateness is transcended. Each is the completion of the other.

In union, other dichotomies in the archetypal imagery of male and female are also resolved. The hardness of male interplays with the softness of female as does their giving and receiving, finding and losing, firmness and yielding. In union, the physiological emptiness of woman is filled by the physiological fullness of man until her emptiness empties his fullness. There is, indeed, a bilateral symmetry in both sexuality and consciousness that is intrinsic in thinking and doing. Union is the enactment of their resolution.

But the way of the Tao also requires that dichotomies not be resolved. As there is the yin of union so there is the yang of separation. What comes together must also come apart. Taoist energies are rhythmical, not linear. The Tao is followed not by holding what is attained but by balancing what inevitably must begin and end, come and go, rise and fall, fill and empty. As well as the togetherness of man and woman, there must also be acknowledgement of their separateness.

Even that separateness, however, is effused with a belonging to the larger pattern of things. We are a self that is separate as well as a belonging that weaves into the full fabric of the whole. We are, at the same time, self and lover and whole.

Explanations are difficult because they are bound to the conventions of language. Language is linear; it wants to dismantle and stretch into sequence experiences that are inherently whole and simultaneous, that are gestalt. Linearity is only a part of the whole.

Language misrepresents in other ways. The Tao, for example, is used grammatically as a noun but it is not to be understood as a noun. It is more gerundial, not noun and not verb. It is neither a thing nor an idea. It is like a quantum wave function, hovering somewhere between thing and idea, a fuzzy noun and an idea unrealized. It is not bound by conceptualizations or untangled by thought. It is not limited by the structure or convention of this writing and thinking. For something to be understood, it must essentially be a substance of thought. The Tao cannot be understood because it is larger than thought. It is process that we can attune to but it is not something that can be understood or separated from living because it is the whole itself.

Loving is similarly elusive exactly because it is us. Loving is process, a changing within changing, a process of relationship that is recognized only because of imagined unchanging and separateness. Loving is relationship and we are relationship and the Tao is relationship. As Relativity Theory points out everything is, in effect, relationship. Loving is the elusive relationship between what is called separateness and togetherness.

The relationship we call loving is as intrinsic to us as heat is to fire, hardness is to stone, wind is to air. But there is no need to become metaphysical and uppity about a quality that we assign exclusively to ourselves. Anthropocentricity is what we might expect of ourselves. We are just as absorbed in being ourselves as tree is absorbed in being tree. All relationship is similarly engrossing. Roots are intent upon soil and water, leaves upon air and sun. Does the flower not await the pollen? The relationship of lover to lover lost in themselves is the same as anything to anything lost in themselves. Everything is absorbed in being what it is and is lost in that absorption.

Lovers, lost in themselves, create their own freedom just as each thing's freedom is its propensity to know and do only what it, itself, is. Being lost in ourselves is the condition we call freedom. At the same time, selflessly, we have no choice but to conform to the larger harmony of things. In the Taoist way of understanding, love is like freedom and should not be treated as an absolute.

Lovers in harmony with each other enact the same principle of relationship with each other that the sage does with the world. They experience an expansiveness and deep accord that they might call freedom or love but which is virtue/power. Lovers freely loving each other engage in the same process with which the Taoist sage moves with the Tao. Thus everything is honoured and each thing seems to fulfill itself.

Lovers are free to be themselves so they can receive themselves. As lovers receive themselves, so everything receives itself. It is, after all, a uni-verse. It is here that lovers are unknowingly Taoists. Lovers, through themselves, have access to the sage's way if they can be large enough to see more widely than the narrow gaze into each other's eyes. The process by which they fulfill themselves is the same as the process by which everything fulfills everything else.

The Taoist's art is to live with the world in a state of mutually erotic fulfillment. Erotic is not just sexual. Erotic means a profound mutuality, a deep balancing of opposites, a dissolving of the edges of things so that everything melds into everything else while remaining itself. For lovers, of course, it is in union that passion and compassion reach the profoundly erotic. For the sage, it is a holistic way of balanced moving with the world while letting it stay balanced with itself.

The balancing of man and woman is the sagely lovers' beginning of a larger process of balancing. When man and woman balance with each other, then there is opportunity for that balance to generalize. The controlling and ruling attributes of yang are balanced with the yielding and nurturing attributes of yin. We take a softer stance in the world and evolve from "mankind" to "humankind."

Great things are accomplished little by little. Although there may be broader implications to the balancing of man and woman, the little task of this book is to deepen and harmonize the male and female energy. Like yin and yang in Taoism, female and male are the two handles of our human reality. As man or woman we must come to terms with ourselves and our sexual counterpart, not only in a physical way but also in a philosophical and aesthetic way.

Just as fish can rely upon water for swimming, so man and woman can rely upon their mutual sexual attraction as a medium for moving more deeply into themselves and the Tao. An increase in mind's awareness of the depth and breadth of sexuality also increases the body's awareness so that physical and mental energy are mutually enhancing. The emphasis in this book is not upon physical sexuality but upon its philosophical and aesthetic dimensions. More weight is needed here to balance a cultural attitude that is tipped toward the thoughtlessly physical. With balancing comes access to the holistic experience of unity.

What is the holistic experience of unity? Words won't say because they do not include body's language. Body won't say because it does not speak with mind's words. But the whole of experience knows when the opposites of male and female, one and other, mind and body wholly come together. Sexual union is a physical union but it is also a symbolic union of archetypal polar opposites; it is both an actuality and a representation of the procreative energy that moves everything toward togetherness. Thus is everything re-charged and re-newed. Sexual union is the inclusion of outside and other into inside and self. Thereby is dissolved inside and outside, self and other.

From this resolution comes again the separating of man and woman, and then the dividing of woman into progeny that in turn unite and divide. And so continues from generation to generation the charged rhythm.

But biology tends to itself. What we need to do is cultivate the art of being both passive and active, of being both used by sexual energy and of being a user of sexual energy. The task is to find a way in which wide-awake body is integrated with a wide-awake and uninterrupting mindfulness, to manoeuvre ourselves to a body and mind position where we are enlarged by the full sexual energy of man and woman. To be fully sexual is to be enriched and charged enough to meet the rich and charged primal that is virtue/power.

Virtue/power is found by moving toward profound confusion until something profoundly confusing happens. So it is that we do not arrive at love but move more profoundly into loving. The Taoist balancing of man and woman is the process of moving more and more deeply into relationship until something profoundly important happens.

The Tao of Relationships

The Tao

1. Practicing for Now

Water does not flow upward to the mountain's separating but downward to the sea's joining. Man and woman are the downward course of each other.

Flow with each other and move together ever downward toward the sea's joining. Be moved, be carried, be taken willingly by the primal urge. It is infallible. From the very beginning it has been practicing for now.

2. Beyond Measure

There is something between man and woman that the five senses cannot find. Listen and there is silence. Smell and taste...nothing. Touch emptiness. Eyes have never seen it. Where is its height and width and depth and weight? Words say it is something yet it cannot be measured.

It is given and not earned, received but not taken. It happens to us and for us and with us, yet it cannot be found.

That which cannot be found cannot be lost. Without measure it is beyond measure.

3. Just Doing

Flowing from the mountain to the sea, the stream touches every stone in its path. Rain wets where it falls; from highest to lowest, from hardest to softest, from dryest to wettest.

Indiscriminate water. It moistens and nourishes everything. Beyond accepting and rejecting, it is even beyond choosing. No will. No struggle. Just doing.

4. By Remaining Still

The gift of the Tao is greater than any gift. How can it be given? By remaining still when others cannot control their giving; by remaining still when others cannot control their taking.

When there are mountains, water flows away from them. When there are valleys, water flows into them.

It is the moving stillness between man and woman that is their greatest gift to each other. Trust the stillness. Be still together and it will move.

5. The Great Allowing

The Great Mother is the living vessel of everything. In everything is the living of herself.

By doing nothing, she permits all things to be. Within her great roundness, the brown and green and creatures flourish of themselves. She herself only is, like a promise to everything, so each thing may do as itself.

Because of the Great Mother, there is a present bond between everything. Round and surrounding, she is the full emptiness in which all takes place. Belonging in everything yet found in nothing, she is the Great Allowing.

6. The Boundless Room

No walls and there is no dwelling place. The room that is too small cannot be lived within. It is the emptiness within that must feel comfortable.

The place that houses a man and woman's togetherness must define but not constrict, enclose yet be spacious. In the dwelling of two together, find the boundless room.

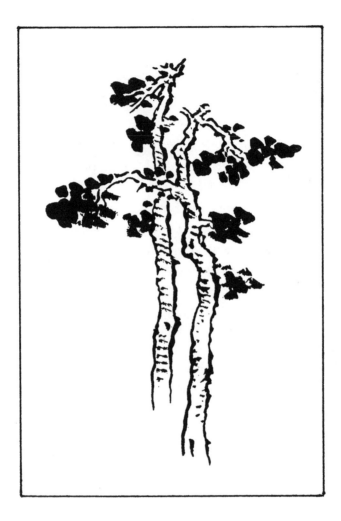

7. To Keep the Bond

To keep the bond that is between man and woman, hold it in awe.

Wear it like wind and sea. Embrace it like mountain.

8. Have Each Other As If

That which is kept will be lost. That which is lost will be kept. Have each other as if there cannot be keeping.

9. Becomes From Within

Possess and there will be loss. Try and there will be failure. Struggle and there will be defeat. To arrive, unloose. To discover, yield. To trust, empty. To receive, honour.

What seems complicated is simple and easily followed because it is not given from without but becomes from within.

10. Not a Mystery

It is called the Tao. Because it is in everything, it is between everything. It is everywhere, in every instant. So it is not a mystery. But search for it and it will be missed. Think about it and there will be confusion.

To smell...just breathe. To hear...just listen. To find...just open. So it is that man and woman do not find each other but are found by each other.

11. Without

Without ears, hear through the silence. Without eyes, see through the darkness. Without words, know the unspoken.

12. Foolish Play

Pretense cannot be maintained, dishonesty forever hidden. Painted faces will be unmasked. Only those who have forgotten they deceive are fooled by deception. For eyes that see, what foolish play!

Where in the universe can anything be hidden? So a little honesty is greater than a thousand cunning deceptions.

13. The Place to Begin

Pretense obscures the obvious. We are not what we pretend to be. Not even effort reveals ourselves. Trying makes matters worse. When effort and pretense are cleared away, that which is itself will of itself become itself. This is the place to begin.

14. The Greatness of Simple

Even though the beginning seems complex, the beginning of the beginning is simple. Find the simple beginning. The greatest arises from the simplest. At the centre of the largest is the smallest. Find the greatness of simple.

Be careful of pretense and adornment. When seeking the important, keep to the simple. Great is never complicated. Trust the simple. Accord and harmony arise from it. Greatest is always found in least.

15. Attend to the Ordinary

Come closer to the common mystery. Attend to the ordinary. There is nothing else to find. All the travelling of thought returns to the beginning and recognizes the obvious. It is wisdom that sees the ordinary with amazement.

16. Balance the Universe

Too loud and we are not heard. Too bright and we are not seen. Too fancy and we are hidden. Too much and we are obscured.

Let speaking come from deep within, from the quiet place. Let silence speak. Listen for silence. Hear the sound between words.

Be patient and attentive. It is the surface that is first apparent. Give time for depth to find depth.

During each moment, balance the universe.

17. Thoughts and Questions

Where do we get new bodies? Each body finally fails; each self is finally lost. The self of each body must acknowledge the humility of its condition.

Now proceed ordinarily. Forget that the greatest dangers are thoughts and questions.

18. Because of Our Changing

The space between man and woman cannot be filled and cannot be emptied. Fill it and there is room for more. Empty it and more remains.

Seek it and it will not be found. Summon it and it will not come. Lose it yet it will not be lost.

Because it is without value, it is beyond value; because it is beyond value, it is given freely. Great effort cannot earn it. Once found, it cannot be contained.

Each moment it is different but it is called the same name because of our changing.

19. Finding is Recognizing

If it is as simple as man and woman meeting each other, why is it so difficult? Such struggle! Such yearning and searching, scheming and wrangling, insisting and beseeching! Such contortions! Something gets in the way and the simple becomes complex.

Finding is recognizing, not making. Wishing and desiring and hoping, even loneliness, are best forgotten for they muddy mind-water.

20. And Its Passing

When things seem difficult, remember the easy and its passing. When things seem easy, remember the difficult and its passing. Thus patience and perspective are kept and complacency is avoided.

21. With the Spoken Question

Stop the moving and examine its changing. Take away from the empty. Add to the full. Name it and lose it in the snare of words. With the spoken question, break the silent answer.

Watch in the darkness. Feel in the emptiness. Listen in the silence.

22. So Obvious

Like the Tao, it is so wide it cannot be missed, so narrow it cannot be found, so obvious it is elusive.

When harmony comes not from subduing or peace from overpowering or quiet from silencing, then it is there.

It is gone when struggling, lost when taking. It is given when receiving, filled when emptying.

23. The Journey to the Beginning

Lose the ordinary to find the ordinary. The unusual affirms the worth of the usual. Leave the familiar to finally know the familiar. All our journeying leads back to the ordinary. It is the ordinary that is extraordinary.

Be pretentious, dress up fancy, and something is both lost and found. Lose without finding and it is easy to be waylaid on the journey to the beginning.

24. The Silent Ground

The simple is overlooked by complexity. The easy is missed by cleverness. It is with difficulty that we make fools of ourselves.

Begin by emptying. Then listen and watch. Listen to the hearing, watch the seeing. With ears wide open, thoughtlessly hear. With eyes wide open, thoughtlessly see. The silent ground will sound. The empty air is full.

The Tao cannot be separated from itself.

25. Practice Humility

Practice humility and do not try to get ahead of each other. A winner requires a loser. Retribution provokes reprisal. What a foolish circle to be trapped within.

We are born in humility and we die in humility. From beginning to end, it is a proven path.

26. Words Are Easy

Words are easy to use but what use are they? The Tao cannot be said. Search every word and not one will do. Call it the Tao but what it is called is not what it is. Where is the Tao? In each word. Between each word. Beyond each word.

Forget words. Follow in the heart the teachings of the sages and then be free of the teachings and the sages. Then there is the Tao.

But remember one word of advice and the Tao is gone. Name one thing and the Tao is missed. Don't even think a word.

27. To Possess the Sky

Stop the water and seize the river. Take hold of the air and possess the sky. Such foolish struggle. To seize the river... become river. To possess the sky...become sky.

28. Effortless As Birth and Death

Each conception and birth enacts the flow of dark to light; each life and death enacts the flow of light to dark.

The day cannot be stopped. The moon will move in its course. The seasons change in their rightful rhythm. Be at peace with the natural order. Accept death as birth was accepted.

Each moment is birth and death. The time is always here when everything releases and we are caried by the Tao.

Timing is crucial. To avoid too early or too late, be both attentive and indifferent. The entire universe hinges on each instant yet not one thing matters. Each moment is as effortless as birth and death.

29. Found by a Way

It is the emptiness between that draws together man and woman. Search for it and it is lost. Pursue it and it is unattainable. To find the emptiness...first empty. Without wanting, without needing, we are found by a way.

30. Meeting Like Water

Beyond strength is yielding and beyond yielding is strength. Answers are beyond questions and questions are beyond answers. Beyond one is other. Beyond both is the Tao.

To understand beyond both, think beyond one and other to wholeness. How can mind be so big? By thinking small. Even in the smallest is the wholeness of the Tao.

How can man and woman get beyond both? By breaking and meeting like water.

31. Having Been for So Long

The primal urge was long before and will be long after. Having been for so long, it cannot fail now. Accept it and live harmoniously within it. It has more than can fulfill two lives.

32. To Find the Tao

Use both feet to walk. Use both ears to hear. Use both eyes to see. To understand, one is not enough. Use both minds to find the Tao.

Mind searching with the mind of self finds only self. Use both the mind of self and not-self for full minding.

Lose self to find not-self. Lose one to find other. Lose both to find the Tao.

33. Every Is

Mind encloses every is with is-not and ends every is-not with is. Only with mind do we divide and know one from other.

With small mind, one is defined by other. With large mind, one belongs with other. With no-mind, one is other.

34. Beneath Each Knowing

There is mystery because there is not-knowing. Yet beneath each knowing is the next not-knowing. So each knowing deepens the mystery.

Yet even in knowing there is the mystery of knowing.

35. The Tao's Way

The Tao's way is to empty when there is too much and to fill when there is not enough. Such is its way.

When mind is too full, it must be emptied. When empty, it will be filled by the Tao.

When man and woman are happily full of each other, they keep the emptiness that balances the fullness. When they are unhappily full of each other and wish together to begin again, they first must empty.

Man / Woman

36. Close to the Great Mother

The sweet is not substantial; the substantial is not sweet. Sustenance bears the flavours of earth.

Keep close to the Great Mother. Where else do we always return? We are the fruits and grains of her. Rooted in her soils we grow where we are. Arising from her we are nurtured and harvested by her wisdom.

Man and woman are living earth. Soiled by her grace we find each other, touch her flesh, drink her nectars, flourish in her simple treasures.

37. Both Halves of Now

There is not man only or woman only. The nature of one makes necessary the other.

How curious to struggle against the way things are. How much wiser to become the way things are.

How large must we become? As big as man and woman. As great as both halves of now.

38. The Fulfillment of Each

Man, alone in his manliness, is incomplete. Woman, alone in her womanliness, is incomplete.

Such eager struggle as each searches to find other so there is both.

So it is that there is man and woman and the fulfillment of each is other.

39. By Unknowing

He, the known, is seeker of the unknown. She, the unknown, is keeper of the unknown.

Unseen, the darkness of the woman's place is the primal origin that lures man beyond knowing to unknowing.

Once there is knowing, the Tao can be found only by unknowing.

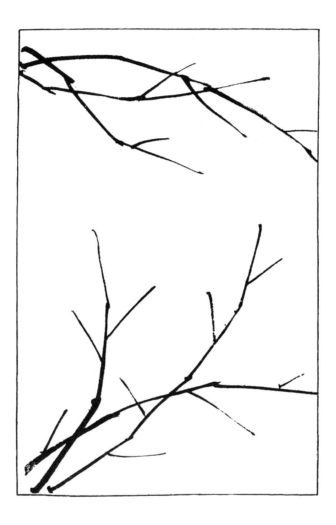

40. Undivided Silence

There has been naming so there has been dividing. Because one follows other, after dividing there will be wholeness. Therefore, name and divide that wholeness may ensue. Call woman the name woman and divide her from man. Call man the name man and divide him from woman. Beyond calling and naming and dividing, find wholeness and undivided silence.

41. Foolish Seriousness

How can man and woman, searching for each other, be peaceful? Such an obsession! Every look sees only searching and the whole world is turned into one need. Hunger grips below the belly, the heart echoes lonely and hollow, and everyone becomes possibility. Such struggle and ritual and turnings! Such foolish seriousness.

42. The Simple and Great

For those who crave goods, remember that the bond between man and woman requires nothing. Having much obscures so that the simple and great are hidden by the passing and trivial.

43. The Other's Hidden Centre

Too much hides not enough. Loudness disguises uncertainty. Hurry misses care. Words conceal confusion. Certainty cloaks shallowness. The complex obscures the simple and the simplistic obscures the profound.

Between too much and not enough is the very centre that is where we are. For man and woman who find each other, they each understand the other's hidden centre that tries to balance with the world.

44. Only As Itself

Great spending and possessions, keeping fashionable, paying attention to everybody else.... What have these to do with just man and woman together? They are burdens that encumber the easy, obstruct the ordinary, obscure the Tao.

Too much is as great a danger as too little. If there is too much, cultivate the austere and honour the simple. Man and woman meet naked and the greatest they do each other comes only as itself.

45. Embraced By Emptiness

That which is not, is emptiness. That which is, is embraced by emptiness. Beyond man is always the woman emptiness of the universe.

Man is always held by emptiness. Do what he will, go where he may, there is no escape from the Great Mother's embrace.

46. Within Her Holding

Round and plentiful, she is curve of hip and depth of promise and rise of nourishment. She is woman earth and wisdom, offering and giving, nurturing and fulfilling.

Hard and sparse, he is rise of strength and reach of search and shape of struggle. He is man mountain and knowledge, making and moving, taking and shaping.

As mountain comes from earth, man comes from woman. Everything comes from the Great Mother in which man, like child, plays so seriously upon her lap and within her holding.

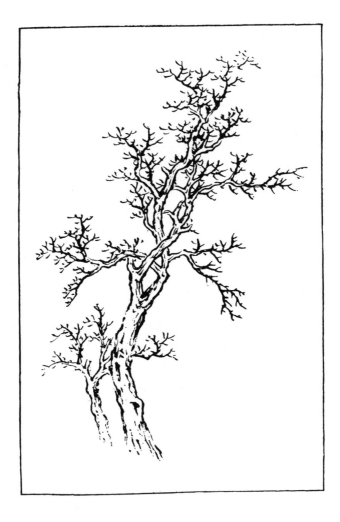

47. Attached By Each Other

Float into the air of idea and disappear into the thin wind of thought. Where then is body that comes from soil and flesh that belongs with flesh?

Touch earth. Smell its fragrance. Taste its flavours. Man and woman are attached by each other to earth.

48. The Trunk and Roots of Words

The tree rises into the enclosing air and the sky enfolds it; its roots descend into the holding soil and the earth nourishes them. Here in union is the moving and the embracing of primal man and woman.

The way to know their union is not with words because they do not catch the at-onceness of motion and stillness, giving and receiving, outer and inner, hardness and softness, holding and yielding.

The trunk and roots of words search up and down between the emptiness of air and the fullness of soil. Thoughts rise and descend with words while the knowing is in the silent embrace of the Great Mother.

49. The Uncommon Man

The flesh that is called man is small in the empty fullness of the Great Mother. The flesh that is called woman possesses emptiness and opens to enfold into itself even the full emptiness of the Great Mother.

It is man with his struggling who tries to change and fill the Great Mother; it is woman with her holding who tries to embrace the Great Mother.

This is why it is difficult for the common man to soften, to empty, to embrace; and why it is only the uncommon man who can be greater than man.

50. Apprenticeships

The apprentice hacks and the wood splinters; the master touches and the wood yields and comes alive.

Even man and woman must serve apprenticeships until they are each one with the other and come alive together.

51. More Easily Found

Who is to be found by woman when a man has not yet found himself? Who is to be found by man when a woman has not yet found herself? Explore and discover that which is within. When we find ourselves, we are more easily found by others.

52. The Sage's Way

Cultivate caution but overcome fear. Balance giving and receiving. Temper urgency with patience. Be servant and master to no one. Follow no one but learn from everyone. Know self and not-self; since inner and outer are each other, full inside requires full outside. Find the sage's way of thinking by doing.

In spite of great distances, there is nowhere to go; in spite of everywhere else in the universe, the answer is here. There are no destinations, only the journey reached wherever we are.

53. The One That Is Both

How foolish that man and woman should try to conquer each other. Be guided not by one or other but by both together. Follow the primal calling and each be humbled before the one that is both.

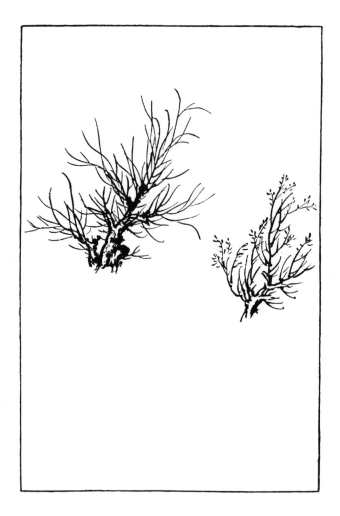

54. Wholeness Again

It is indeed propitious that the halfness of man and the halfness of woman should each be completed by the halfness of other. Halves are united and incompletes completed. In the losing of each into both and one, there is wholeness again.

55. That Each May Be Greater

What is greater than the union of the opposites called man and woman? Woman completes man and man completes woman. Each is lost that each may be greater than man or woman alone. Inside and outside are gone, self and not-self resolved. Two become one while remaining two.

56. Enter the Between

Trust what is between man and woman. Although it is present, it will not be commanded; although it is summoned, it will not come.

Without wish or want or thought, enter the between of man and woman. When quietly there, gently open and be carried by the primal urge.

57. When There is the Tao

When the drop of water releases and the great river flows, there is the Tao. When the spring bud opens and the autumn leaf falls, there is the Tao.

When there is the Tao between man and woman, it is like the morning sun rising by itself.

58. But Silently Laugh

From the still place within, how foolish seems the seeking of man and woman for each other. How can it be taken seriously? The glances and whispers, the asking and urging, the trading of self for self.

Yet there is such relief when two see clearly into each other and the search is called finished.

From the still place and the death bed, what can be done but silently laugh. Such seriousness ending in foolishness; such foolishness ending in seriousness.

59. The Primal is Tamed

Within each man is all men; within each woman is all women. When a man opens himself to himself and finds he is all men, he is closer to the primal. And when a woman opens herself to herself and finds she is all women, she is closer to the primal.

As one man, open to become all men; as one woman, open to become all women. Become uncommon. Beneath the uncommon is a deeper common.

When a man who is all men meets a woman who is all women, the primal is mounted. When the man knows the woman as all women and the woman knows the man as all men, the primal is tamed.

60. Primal Dark

Woman is the possessor of secret dark and emptiness. She is the luring huntress of light and man's fullness who fills her emptiness and reveals the secret.

In her primal dark is the deep origin and secret wisdom for which man searches. She is the receiver of him and the bearer of his wisdom.

In woman, man finds what is beyond thinking's struggle.

61. Man's Death in Woman

Woman is the generous and welcoming valley of soft mountains where man willingly comes from the hardness of the world to be overcome.

She is warm promise and roundness of full earth and moon to which even the wisdom of heaven is left speechless.

She is the presence of primal beginning from which man arises. Birth and life struggle him away but desire and death enchant him back.

A man's death in woman is his birth again.

She is confirmation of the small and great rhythms of blood and generations to which he keeps returning for comfort and release.

62. Is–Not Is As Great As Is

No woman is only woman; no man is only man. Without the woman in man and the man in woman, there would be no understanding between man and woman.

Yet it is the not-man in woman that makes for man her mystery and allure; and it is the not-woman in man that makes for woman his mystery and allure. Is-not is as great as is.

63. Serious Riddle

It is dangerous for man and woman with their power of male and female, to be together in the Great Breathing.

While holding to the centre, they must move with the breathing and bend with the forces or they break and lose their togetherness or even their separateness. While holding fast, they must let go; while letting go, they must hold fast. While together, they must be separate; while separate, they must be together.

What is twoness and oneness, other and self, losing and keeping, more and less, strength and vulnerability, fruition and beginning? What serious riddle is this?

64. Each Body's Other Body

The distant pleasing of eyes does not promise the approval of the other senses. They must confirm what smiles at eyes.

When bodies belong, all the senses are charmed by each body's other body. New yet familiar, separate yet belonging, each other's body is different and the same.

When a man and woman come home to their own other body, there is the Tao.

65. The Tao Is Like Nothing

Just as words can only be understood from outside the structure of words, thinking can only be understood from outside the structure of thinking. Everything requires something else to be understood. Where will this kind of thinking lead?

Man understands man through woman; woman understands woman through man. To understand man-and-woman, something else is needed. Something else needs something more. Something more needs everything. To understand everything, understand nothing.

The Tao is like nothing; an unsaid word, an unthought thought. Because of words, we think there is the Tao but it is not a word, not a thought.

66. Without Words

Words have divided man from woman, one from other, this from that until only sages know how to put things together.

Without words, without even understanding, lovers find each other.

67. Broad Harmony

In all the wide and intricate earth where everything comes from everything else, there can be nothing other than broad harmony. Sun shines. Rain falls. Mountains rise from valleys. Streams flow seaward. Earth breathes its rhythms and there is the beginning called birth and death.

Harmony is everywhere, so ordinary...it is commonly missed.

In the great accord, each detail belongs. Thus, the sage attends to the particular but is guided by the general. There is no need to condemn disasters or praise miracles. Even man and woman...just extraordinarily ordinary.

68. Silently Certain

There are uncertain eyes that glance to others to find the knowing that they themselves must see.

There are things that only we alone can know. We are each the secret seers whose deep looking into each other we ourselves must do.

When a man and woman are silently certain, the bond of their own finding will be recognized by those who see, and going their own way, quite indifferently, others will bend to their knowing.

69. Letting Go

Proceed together as man and woman while balancing each and other.

To balance, let go of man and find woman, let go of woman and find man; let go of each and find other, let go of other and find each.

Then, while holding each and letting go of both, see both clearly. While holding both and letting go of each, see each clearly.

70. If Man Wanted Only Light

If man wanted only light, he would not close his eyes and lie with woman and enter the gate of darkness. Those who want only simple understanding would not court darkness and woman.

As there is great blindness in light, there is great seeing in darkness. Out of darkness all seeing begins. The moist darkness of woman is the source of light, the primordial place from which came beginning and to which end returns.

Those who want only light will not understand beginnings and endings, comings and goings, the great tides in all things.

When man comes to woman, he comes to a special darkness.

71. From Easiness With the Ordinary

Great mountains do not cover the entire earth; waterfalls are not the whole river. Most of the extraordinary is ordinary.

Man and woman grow together in the rhythms of the everyday; daily chores, comfortable silence, desires rising and fulfilled.

From easiness with the ordinary, togetherness comes quietly in the shared and simple commonplace.

72. Young Lovers' Riddles

In the cool pines where the air is sharp and thin, what would the old sage say? Is the old man, wandering his way up the mountain, spared the dilemma of lovers?

What would he do when every thought of his mind said "No!" and every muscle of his body said "Yes!"

Aging blood cools some heat for which there was not time or urge to deliberate. Perhaps the sage just ages into his wisdom.

How can wise old men be the solvers of young lovers' riddles?

Separateness / Togetherness

73. Arises From Itself

If only ones were needed, there would not be twos. Yet each one of us arises out of the two who unite into one.

In man and woman there is something other than man and woman, something that arises from itself, that seeks itself and grows out of itself.

It is so easy it cannot be earned, so close it is rarely noticed.

74. With Beginning and End Clear

When searching for another to make two, remember the nature of one; we are born by ones and we die by ones.

With beginning and end clear, find balance. From balance comes patience and harmony.

75. Easy Silence

When words hide silence, listen to silence and not to words.

Easy words are the silence of companionship. Easy silence speaks well of togetherness.

76. Empty and Full

Meeting is the beginning of separating; separating is the beginning of meeting. When is there only leaving and when is there only arriving? Separate start from finish, this from that, one from another.

One arises out of other. So at the same time, remember and forget.

Whatever happens is surprising and unexpected. The unforeseen is recognized and awaited.

Whether separate or together, proceed empty and full, knowing and not-knowing. Thus balance and harmony ensue.

77. Hiding

Hiding one whole self from another whole self encumbers full meeting.

It is difficult enough for naked bodies to meet wholly.

When two selves are clothed in pretense, they cannot come together; there is separateness in their togetherness, not togetherness in their separateness.

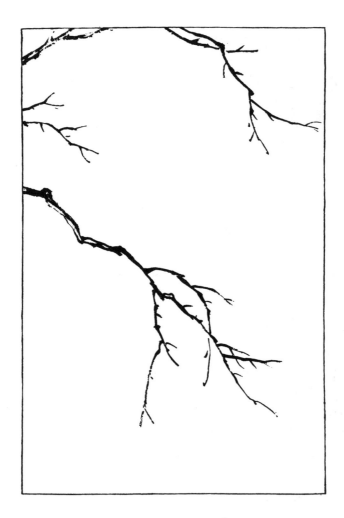

78. In the Stillness of Right Time

Separateness falls away like leaves from the autumn maple.

It is no use to shake the tree when the leaves are still green.

Even in the stillness of right time, branches are slowly bared and become naked with each other.

79. Separate Without Separateness

We have forgotten that looking came from seeing and listening came from hearing. Separateness came from togetherness.

For looking to again become seeing and listening to again become hearing, fill looking with looking and listening with listening until looking and listening are full and easy.

Then look at the looking, listen to the listening. Empty thought from eye and ear. Look without looking and there is seeing; listen without listening and there is hearing.

Separate without separateness and there is togetherness.

80. Most Together

Gone when remembered and there when forgotten, the Tao keeps eluding direct mind.

Man and woman are most together when unaware of their togetherness; like unfelt shoes that ease the walking, like unnoticed coats that keep away the chill, they unknowingly wear each other.

81. One Thing Comes from Another

The sages say that one thing comes from another. Woman arises out of man and man arises out of woman.

The outside always begins in the inside. Man finds woman by first finding himself and woman finds man by first finding herself. Begin with self to find *other*.

Togetherness arises out of separateness. To find togetherness, begin with separateness. In this way there can be both togetherness and separateness.

82. Crooked And Round

Togetherness and separateness together; separateness and togetherness separate. How are two to become one while remaining two? Where is separateness within togetherness and togetherness within separateness?

Join together when there is separateness and break apart when there is togetherness. While keeping oneness, use twoness; while keeping twoness, use oneness.

Mind's questions play with words. The confusion is always single mind trying to think straight. The Tao's crooked and round and many ways do not conform to thinking's play.

There are no questions to ask so do not ask. There are no answers to give so do not answer. Play without questions, without answers.

83. Right Mind

One mind alone will not understand the wholeness of togetherness. Two minds together will not understand the wholeness of separateness.

One mind and two minds and many minds are needed. Each understanding requires right mind.

Where then is whole-mind and no-mind?

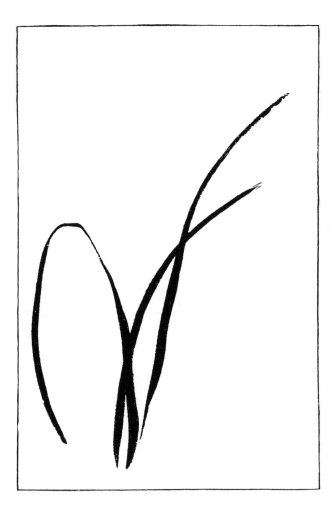

84. In Each Two

When a man and woman are alone and united, they are unique in their togetherness with each other but common in their sameness with others.

In each two are two becoming one; in each two are all becoming one. What binds together each two, binds together every two and binds together all. In each two all is made understandable.

For each two...all is found. Through each two...the Tao is found. Embrace each other and all is embraced. How else could the Tao be embraced?

85. Third Mind

In the separateness of two minds is a third mind that knows togetherness.

Neither mind can explain what is third mind but each mind hears it when listening to togetherness. It is something inside that understands outside, something outside that understands inside. It is how inside meets outside, how one meets *other*, how each becomes both.

Third mind cannot be grasped, cannot be resisted. By the losing that finds, it comes of itself in its own time.

86. Seed And Soil

Man and woman grow out of each other. Each is seed and soil of the other.

When there is urge and strength and change, seed each other and be the conceiving father. When there is patience and caring and peace, feed each other and be the nourishing mother.

Out of seed and soil promise arises.

87. Finding

If those who are alone and separate are so needy of another and togetherness, why is it so difficult for the needy to find the needy?

Are there just a few amid many whom we can choose or is there just one amid few? Is it ourselves we seek outside ourselves? Who is it that we seek? Questions chase questions. Thinking confuses seeking.

Seeking seems difficult. Finding seems easy.

Just as searching creates looking that prevents seeing, needing creates seeking that prevents finding.

Finding is the opening that recognizes.

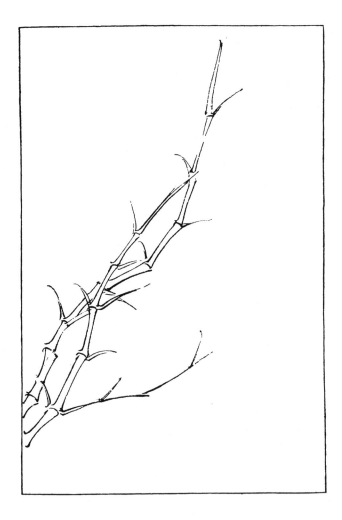

88. The Obvious That Is the Secret

It is the ordinary that is extraordinary. How ordinary that man and woman should search out each other and take within each the other as first partner and mate! How ordinary that knowing one's self is the way to knowing another! How ordinary that wonder grows with familiarity, that mystery enlarges with understanding, that gaining increases with losing! How ordinary that man and woman, made certain and uncertain by their togetherness, are unmade and remade, lost and new-found!

To understand the ordinary, thinking is useless. Choice and no-choice, doing and not-doing, why and why-not struggle to a bewildering stalemate.

It is the obvious that is the secret. The ordinary is the extraordinary hidden in the ordinary. The extraordinary Tao is just the ordinary Tao.

89. One-Legged Mind

Why do separateness and togetherness breathe each other in and out? Why do man and woman dance for something more than themselves?

Mind searches but something fundamental keeps eluding unbreathing mind, one-legged mind.

90. Secret Meeting Secret

Some of body's parts are openly and proudly displayed, some are clothed by decorum and some other parts are hidden until each man and woman's special meeting. Then two bodies touch and share and open toward the full knowing of each other.

When man and woman know each other and are no longer bound by modesty or propriety or constraint, when all that can be opened is opened and there is nothing left to hide, something remains hidden, something remains secret.

What is it that seems to lie just beyond the reach of touching and knowing, that enchants touching and knowing, that enlivens body's thinking and mind's parts, that makes each man and woman secret meeting secret?

91. Rely On the Effortless

Be with each other but do not possess each other. Grasping loses. Togetherness comes of itself. In daily affairs, tend to little things and great problems are overcome. Deal with trouble before it begins. Master the ordinary and the extraordinary comes easily. Trust the simple and find it in the complicated. Expect the difficult and things will be easy. Be attentive but rely on the effortless.

92. To Be Within Both

From togetherness arises remembrance of separateness that unsettles togetherness. From separateness arises remembrance of togetherness that unsettles separateness.

Togetherness includes separateness. Separateness includes togetherness. Within each there is the other.

To be within both, be taken by one and then by the other and then by both together.

But just as there is both that escapes either, there is neither that escapes both.

93. To Lose and Find Both

When there is togetherness and separateness is remembered, togetherness is lost. When there is separateness and togetherness is remembered, separateness is lost. Because of remembering's dividing, if there is not separateness there is togetherness and if there is not togetherness there is separateness.

Take hold of both to let go of both to lose and find both. Take hold of everything to let go of everything. And suddenly...so simple.

94. Finding Its Own Course

The raindrop pierces the stone. The cloud cleaves the mountain.

Confined by the walls of the valley, the stream flows freely, finding its own course.

95. As Easy As Being Found

If man and woman try to be together and struggle for accord and balance, togetherness is so much and so difficult. If they are found by togetherness, they move and open everywhere, everything seems to do itself and togetherness is so much and so easy.

Because we are self, we try for togetherness; because we are not-self, we are taken by togetherness.

Therefore, trust and risk, open and build, then break with fullness into both separateness and togetherness.

Try but also let go. Empty and fill into the impossibility of togetherness. So difficult and as easy as being found.

96. Deep Meeting

The touching of one by another is the inside of each touching the inside of other by outside touching outside. By outside finding outside, inside finds inside.

The one who is outside is taken inside by outside and two insides meet.

When inside has met inside, it is difficult to separate inside from outside.

Is there really inside and outside? Words complicate the simplicity of deep meeting.

97. Quite Enough

Rather than searching everywhere, search more deeply within and within togetherness.

Once the beginning is found, the mystery in each man or woman is quite enough.

98. With No Effort

Togetherness came from before beginning. It came from deeper than within. It harmonizes inside and outside. It resolves the difference in man and woman.

Trust the Tao that is togetherness. Amid the usual and the unusual, each day something more falls away until, with no effort, everything moves in its proper way.

99. With Mind Wide Open

To be both separate and together, just pull mind in half and let thoughts tumble from each side, falling and disappearing, emptying into nowhere.

Lose nerve, hold tight, and something is lost.

Quickly now, with mind wide open and thoughts spilling into emptiness, let go of one and other, both and neither. Let go of each and all, is and is-not, are and are-not.

Without thoughts...be found by the Tao.

Without separateness...be separate. Without togetherness...be together.

100. Between Thoughts

Words say separate and together but what thinking-thought would be indifferent when thought's own choices are bound by words to choose? What thinking-thought would trust the shape of words to shape its thought?

Words follow words thoughtlessly then thoughts follow thoughts by words' same habit. What thought would trust a thought that took the shape of what words say?

Find thoughts not bound by the shape of words. Between thoughts bound by words are boundless thoughts free of words. So no separate, no together, just something quite beyond words.

Hardness / Softness

101. Between Birth and Death

At birth, as the first act, the new body is entrusted to others. At death, as the last act, the old body is entrusted to others.

It is then appropriate that between birth and death there should be a special humility.

102. Winning and Losing

Avoid confrontation, hardness meeting with hardness. The soft voice is heard long after the shout. Gentleness is stronger than anger.

Winning is a kind of losing and losing is a kind of winning. If there must be winning and losing, treat them as the same.

103. Because of Their Softening

Hardness will not join with hardness because each insists upon itself. So it is that man and woman come together because of their softening.

The softening of man and woman is necessary for their balancing; it is the softness they find that assures their togetherness and the hardness they keep that assures their separateness.

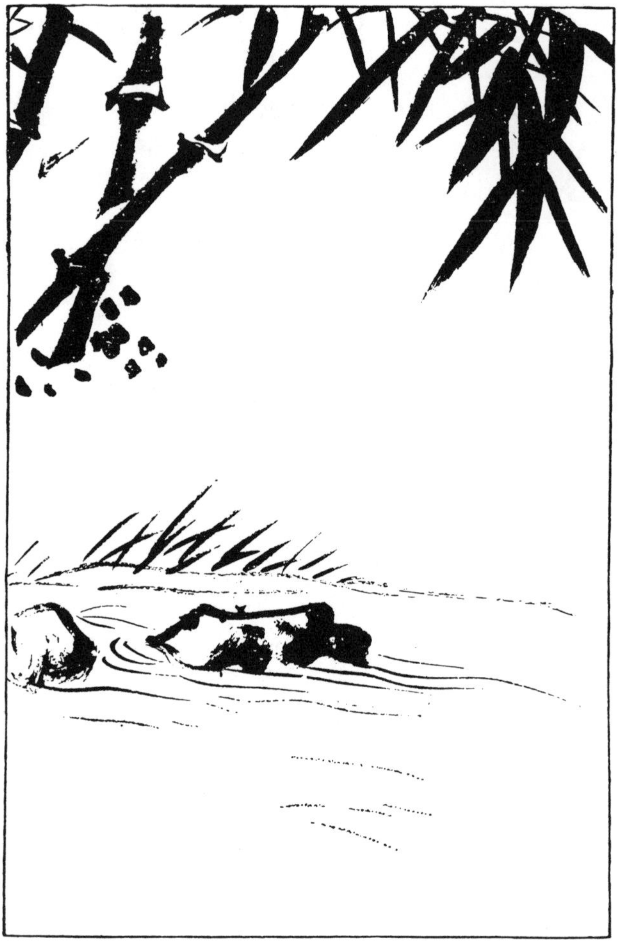

104. Deep Quiet

We grow from a deep silence and are nourished by an enduring quiet.

Great shouts that shock and dismay become unheard noise. But quiet words enter deeply and become the sustenance of each day. Invisible like clear water, hushed like little streams, they nurture, become close companions and great teachers. Speak quietly and listen to the deep quiet within each other.

105. The Wisdom In Everything

The hardness of man is enclosed by the softness of woman and the softness of woman is filled with the hardness of man; this is the way the whole universe meets itself.

Within hardness is the wisdom that knows softness. With just enough softness, man's hardness meets woman and understands her softness. Within softness is the wisdom that knows hardness. With just enough hardness, woman's softness meets man and understands his hardness.

Softness in hardness and hardness in softness is the wisdom in everything. It is the way inside understands outside, here touches there, one comprehends other, this knows that.

106. Softening

oftening permits fullness within to flow out. Softening permits full entering of outside to inside.

107. To Be Used

It is said that hardness restrains and softness permits. Yet there is too hard and too soft, too much and not enough; there is softness that restrains and hardness that permits. Where then is their balance so that man and woman are right with each other?

Fish cannot move in the frozen stream or swim in the morning mist. Roots cannot pierce the solid stone or hold in the blowing sand. Yet into the lightest air birds rise and rest content upon the hardest earth.

As man and woman, do not ask how to use hardness and softness but, together in humility, be used by them. To be used, keep hardness but be softness; keep softness but be hardness.

Be fish and flowing stream, root and waiting earth; be bird and air and even stone.

108. Between Hardness and Softness

The bond that is between man and woman is softness that is hard and hardness that is soft. While it yields to change, it holds man and woman to each other; while it bends them to each other, it holds them firmly together.

In the very centre between hardness and softness, where man and woman yield but are firm, there is a living stillness of bending and unbending.

109. The Softness of Beginning

Within woman, man finds softness and womb, and the great warm ocean of beginning, and the source before himself from which he himself was overcome by birth and hardening.

Lost within the ocean of woman, man returns to the softness of beginning before there was the hardness of himself to struggle against.

This is how the softness of woman overcomes the hardness of man and why the hardness of man seeks out the overcoming softness.

110. Ocean Womb

Woman, overcome as man by birth and hardening, carries within herself the reminder and promise of softness.

Born into hardness, her body grows the ocean womb of soft beginning. She cannot forget or be forgotten when her body reminds.

111. Different Equals

The softness of woman, when tempered with hardness, cannot be overcome; the hardness of man, when tempered with softness, cannot be broken.

Strengthen woman with hardness and moving that she may find understanding in water and man; strengthen man with softness and waiting that he may find understanding in earth and woman.

When there is balance, man and woman will meet as different equals. He will be to her the strength of waiting water and she will be to him the strength of moving earth.

112. Through His Hardness

Man should know that his hardness overcomes the softness and emptiness of woman.

With her softness and emptiness, woman seeks man for his strength and hardness to fill and strengthen and subdue herself.

Man comes to softness through her softness; woman comes to strength through his hardness.

113. Through Her Softness

Woman should know that her softness overcomes the strength and hardness of man.

With his strength and hardness, man seeks woman for her softness and emptiness to empty and soften and subdue himself.

Woman comes to strength through his hardness; man comes to softness through her softness.

114. Hardness Is the Burden

Hardness is the burden that each man and woman must learn to balance with softness.

Even strength needs the wisdom to yield.

Opposition comes from hardness. Hardness requires yielding. Yielding requires strength. Strength requires balance.

Without softness, hardness is a source of trouble; without hardness, softness is a source of trouble.

115. By Emptying

Nothing is lost by emptying. The cup that empties to receive is still the cup; its form remains and its identity is intact. Only its condition changes so that it may receive.

The twofold yielding of man and woman to each other is the softening from which comes emptying and receiving.

Emptying allows the filling of each by other and the making of together.

116. Leading From Behind

At first do not lead. In the beginning it is better that man and woman follow each other.

From following comes leading by following. This is a soft leading, a special kind of leading from behind.

From softness arises humility. From humility arises trust. From trust arises togetherness and one mind.

One mind cannot follow or lead itself. Free from opposites, there is neither leading nor following.

117. Find Awe

Find awe, not fear. Fear is tightness that makes brittle, that hardens and restrains, burdens and confines. Fear creates hardness then separation and breaking.

In fear there cannot be trust and opening, flowing and releasing, giving and coming to oneness.

Trust is softening that opens into awe.

118. Both Hardness and Softness

The valley stones direct the stream. The mountain rocks shed the rain. Falling pebbles part water.

Why is it that, at first, softness gives way to hardness but hardness finally gives way to softness?

If there is a name to say the way things just are, it might be called the Great Allowing or the Great Changing, even the Great Mother. Or just call it the Tao.

The Tao requires both hardness and softness. So for man...keep male but cultivate female. For woman...keep female but cultivate male.

119. Beyond Every Stone

Be held by hardness but rely on softness. Hardness is self that defines and limits; softness is not-self that opens and allows.

Created by hardness, quarrels are resolved by softness.

In streams, water finds its way beyond every stone.

120. Neither Stone nor Water

It is said that water is soft and stone is hard. Yet in the softness of water is something unyielding that erodes the hardness of stone. In the hardness of stone is something yielding that gives way to the softness of water. Find the hardness in water and the softness in stone.

We deceive ourselves when we are stone feigning hardness to water or water feigning softness to stone.

We are outside of words. We are neither stone nor water, hardness nor softness, but just the Tao, taking every form and unable to find even itself.

121. Be Without Purpose

Water does not consider, "Now I will flow here, then I will flow there." Flowing does of itself.

In waterfalls that thunder and in little ponds of silence, water does not intend. There is no purpose in the urge that moves it when it moves.

The secret is this: soften like water, trust the inner urge; leave each moment to itself and move in the unerring course; be without purpose.

Changing / Unchanging

122. Let the Changing Change

Something in a river's changing does not change. The water moves but there is an unchanging that is always present for its own becoming and passing.

Know that all is changing but also that the changing is the All. Trust the unchanging in all changing.

To be the changing, change. To be the unchanging, let the changing change.

123. In Its Proper Time

In its proper time, rain becomes stream, stream becomes river, river becomes sea.

We each flow our own downward way. How can it matter if we are rain or stream, river or sea?

But divide stream from river, even rain from sea, and trouble begins.

Words separate and make unchanging what is together and changing. It is only unchanging mind that struggles to understand.

Without words...find each other.

124. Ever Becoming

Water is not rooted in the earth or anchored in the air of heaven. Attached nowhere, it is everywhere.

That which changes lasts. That which is born takes shape. Taking shape, it is vulnerable. Being vulnerable, it cannot last.

When the bond between man and woman is ever changing, it is ever becoming. Ever becoming, it is ever renewing and ever vital. Water-shaped, it is everywhere, true to itself and the universe.

125. The Downward Way

The course of the inner river is downward. Its way is to find strength in yielding, fulfillment in softening, belonging in accord.

Like the downward way of water, follow the descending course to find a place playfully even among the hardness of rocks.

By this flowing, with changing and unchanging river silently within, outside becomes inside.

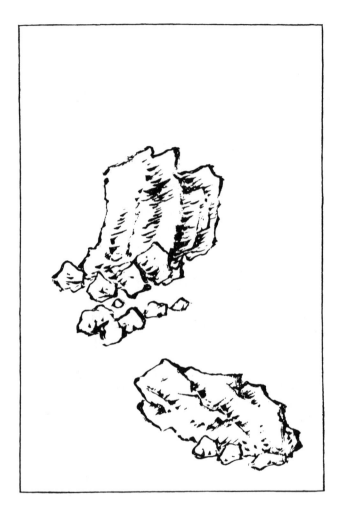

126. Trust the Returning

The unchanging will not last; that which lasts is not unchanging.

The bond as big as mountain for all to admire looms like a monument to falling. It cracks by sun and ice and scatters in broken pieces. It even dissolves in gentle rain. And who can live warm and easy in its shadow?

The bond that lingers like a mist is always waiting in the air, whetting and touching and nourishing. What is more enduring than mist that, changing and unchanging, appearing and re-appearing, gently moistens valley and mountain to living green!

It is better to cultivate the subtle than the conspicuous; better to trust the returning than the constant.

The making is more lasting than the made. Trust what nourishes growing and in the primal promise of growing be nourished.

127. Each Time Has

Each time has its own time. Push and it is too early; hold back and it is too late. At the right time there will be no stopping.

128. A Special Kind of Keeping

Clouds cannot be held. Streams cannot be stopped. New growth will rise from the living root.

Losing, yielding, releasing...each is a special kind of keeping.

129. In the Very Centre of Now

What futility to say, as jealous lovers say of their lover's early lovers, "If only this had not been."

Each life is a growing body that cannot be ordered or divided into pieces that belong or do not belong. It is full of itself, whole without less or more. Denial of part is denial of all. Acceptance releases everything to be what it already is.

By remembering, all of the past is held present by a mind not here.

Every instant is different and belongs, equal in its unalterable filling of moment, in its making whole each now. In the very centre of now is a fullness that even changes unchanging then.

130. Know Like Water

Water changes shape and even form but keeps its essence. River changes water and even course but keeps its essence.

Trust the unchanging in changing. Be water and river, moving and staying, changing and unchanging. Know and soften. Soften and change. Change and endure.

Know like water. Think like river.

131. Also Be River

Everything changes into something else. How futile then to struggle against the passing of what is! In the ever changing of becoming and passing, how can effort be serious? Better to live within the changing. Better to know of the Tao and not-doing.

Not-doing is like the flowing stillness of a river. Be still like the river while the water changes. Be the stillness while changing goes its proper way.

The Tao is river and doing is water. Be water but also be river, always present for changing. Even the waterfall is peaceful.

132. Become Changing

The ancient sages taught, "Yield and be whole. Bend and overcome. Empty and be full."

The hard and unbending are broken by change; the supple and yielding give way and prevail.

For man and woman together, hold fast to unchanging and there will be breaking; become changing, bending in the rhythm of arising and passing, and remain unbroken in a changing stillness.

133. Through Is Between

Returning requires leaving. Stopping needs going. Releasing follows holding. Since each arises from other, then speak to find silence, change to know unchanging, empty to become full.

From moment to moment, mind tricks mind and thoughts follow thinking in circles. The way out is in. The way in is out. Through is between.

Take hold of both halves and swing the doors of mind wide open or closed shut. Full mind is the same as empty mind.

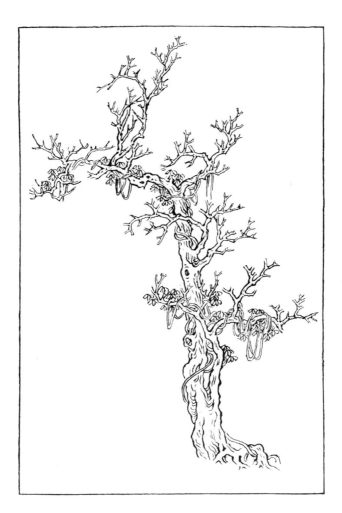

134. The Riddle Called Thinking

Words held upon the page cannot respond with the rightness of now. Thoughts fixed within the mind cannot understand all that is changing. How can changing thoughts understand what is unchanging?

In the riddle called thinking, which thoughts are changing and which are unchanging? Do changing thoughts become unchanging? Do unchanging thoughts change? Are forgotten unchanging thoughts remembered unchanged?

In the tangle of changing and unchanging, how do we find each other? Where do changing thoughts search for changing us? How do unchanging thoughts know changing us?

In the riddle called thinking, if thoughts do not understand themselves, how are we to know each other?

Between changing and unchanging we are together...without a word, without a thought.

Finding/Losing

135. Lose and Find

There is not finding until there is losing. Man losing himself in woman...finds. Woman losing herself in man...finds.

There is not losing until there is finding. Man finding himself in woman...loses. Woman finding herself in man...loses.

It is finding that is losing and losing that is finding. Therefore, find and lose, lose and find.

136. Between One and Other

Something with a primal insistence urges man and woman to each other. Though it cannot be found, it is ever present; though it cannot be lost, it is never found.

It is something between one and other that reconciles separateness; something that is nothing and everything. It is emptiness filling itself until there is finding; fullness emptying itself until there is losing.

Never man without woman or woman without man, it declares that there be both one and other, found and lost in each other.

137. Knowing Deepens

Seeing into eyes is a special touching. At first, eyes avert close touching with eyes.

Seeing is a special touching so naked bodies avoid eyes until there is a special trusting.

What remains to hide when man and woman follow eyes to touch each other with all the senses?

Knowing deepens until the other becomes one's self and an even greater mystery.

138. Into Deeper Unknown

How can one know another? The unfolding of one to another opens the known into deeper unknown.

The only finding is losing that follows losing into the Tao.

139. The Moment of Finding

The moment of finding is always a surprise, like meeting an old friend never before known.

140. Another Knowing

There is a time approved by urge when thought gives way to flesh and mind is beholder of another knowing.

Thoughts cannot meet the needs of flesh until the body thinks. Losing mind and finding body is the beginning of a deeper balance.

Not until there is feeling mind and thinking body will the earthen needs of the secret provinces harmonize the whole kingdom.

141. Losing and Finding

Where is man when he is lost in woman and where is woman when she is lost in man? Where is each when there is no longer separateness?

By being lost, man finds himself again and woman finds herself again. And each, when found in lost, is greater from the losing and the finding.

First there is losing in finding and then finding in losing. The losing in finding is a greater losing and the finding in losing is a greater finding. Follow greater losing and finding.

142. The Lost and Found Way

For man and woman, losing each into other is the way each finds other. By losing they find the togetherness that fulfills each separateness. Lost in each other...they are togetherness; lost in each and other...they are separateness.

Man and woman are the lost and found way everything is together. Therefore, lose without losing, find without finding.

143. Lost in Each Other

When lovers are lost in each other, man is lost in woman and woman is lost in man. Woman, in whom man is lost, is not because she is lost in him; and man, in whom woman is lost, is not because he is lost in her.

This is the mutual illusion of lovers: he thinks that she is when she is not, and she thinks that he is when he is not. Yet how can he think that she is unless he is, and how can she think that he is unless she is, unless he doesn't think he is and so isn't and she doesn't think she is and so isn't. Then he is lost in himself and she is lost in herself.

How do lovers proceed in what is and is not and yet is, and is not and is and yet is not?

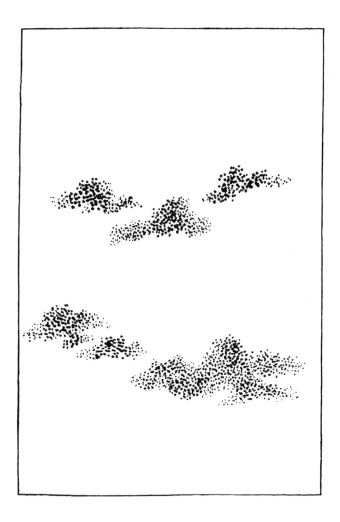

144. Within Between

There is something between man and woman, between birth and death, between one thought and another that thoughts do not understand. Between changing and unchanging, between each and every word, there is something that thoughts cannot know.

Within between, thoughts fall out of thinking.

Done and undone by itself, thinking follows thinking into thoughtlessness.

To find thinking, let go of thoughts.

Finding by losing is also man and woman's way. Unable to understand, no longer even thinking, finally they know.

Giving / Receiving

145. Find Without Taking

ive and there is giving. Receive and there is receiving. But there cannot be having by taking.

Seek without expecting. Find without taking.

146. Full of Emptiness

Fullness cannot receive so begin by emptying. There cannot be full growth without full room. To grow and fill, continue to empty so there can always be receiving.

Be full of emptiness. Emptiness is the greatest receiver. Fullness is the greatest giver.

147. Give Gently

It is not easy to receive, to unfold and open, to trust and accept yet remain one and whole within the spell of another. So giving must account for the burden of receiving.

If there is to be giving, give gently so giver and receiver are lightened.

Receiving is a kind of giving. Give as if receiving and receive as if giving.

148. A Kind of Giving

Clouds do not exact payment from grasses for the worth of rain. Trees are not indebted to sun for the wealth of warmth. Moon and stars are free to the eyes.

So man and woman are free to each other. How can there be debt when giving is the gift of itself and receiving is a kind of giving?

149. Into One Disappears

When she receives, there are two givings; when he gives, there are two receivings. In her opening and receiving, there is giving by receiver; in his entering and giving, there is receiving by giver.

When giving is receiving and receiving is giving, why divide into two that which is one?

Just as giving and receiving disappear into one, into one disappears man and woman, self and other, question and answer.

150. Outside That is Inside

Together in the Tao, man and woman nourish each other like two parts of the same body. Nothing is asked yet all is given and received thoughtlessly. Each is the other's outside that is inside attending to both.

151. To Receive

To receive, be fullness but cultivate emptiness. Fullness is what others know as body and thought, the vessel to which there can be giving; emptiness is the unknown within that receives what is given.

It is what is that gives; it is what is not that receives.

Be only full and there is no emptiness that receives. Be only empty and there is no one who receives. To receive, find emptiness within fullness.

Find fullness that cannot be emptied by giving and find emptiness that cannot be filled by receiving.

152. The Vitality of Riddles

As master...it serves. As shadow...it leads. As one's own...it cannot be kept. To have it...surrender it. To use it...give it. To subdue it...submit to it.

We are the vitality of riddles. Therefore, know without solving.

When riddles to solve become riddles to live, live their vitality. Except...no questions, no answers.

153. Giving and Receiving

There is the great hardness of man seeking to fill and the great softness of woman seeking to hold. How gracious that there is hardness to be held by her softness and softness to encompass his greatness.

She is receiver, receiving with her giving and giving with her receiving. He is giver, giving with his receiving and receiving with his giving.

So it is with man and woman that because of hardness and softness, filling and holding, giving and receiving are the same.

154. Some Great Matter

When giving and receiving are one, what is the name of that one? What name could be given that would speak it? It is something words cannot catch.

How long will words give chase? The words that keep trying set more words running. And the one urge is missed with different words chasing in silly circles. Words are what more words seek.

There is a primal something of which we are each, with bird and fish and tree and stone, source and consequence.

During the moments of union, some great matter is being tended to for which words are audience to the echo.

Fullness / Emptiness

155. Find What Is Not

The emptiness from before birth follows the living years into death, receiving all the fullness between.

Somewhere in each man and woman there is an emptiness that receives the fullness of the other.

To receive what is, find what is not.

After finding the emptiness, find the stillness that receives moving and changing.

156. Remember Emptiness

As man, fill happily with woman. As woman, fill happily with man. As thinker, fill happily with thoughts. But do not forget emptiness.

While filling to fullness with our most amazing selves, remember emptiness. It is emptiness that surrounds lover and ourselves and everything.

Fullness can arise only from emptiness. No emptiness...no fullness.

Emptiness is the ground from which all arises, to which all returns.

157. Begin By Emptying

Man and woman are words and thoughts shaped by mind's thinking. What mind invents, thoughts confirm. But there is something between man and woman that keeps escaping thoughts, that the shape of mind's understanding cannot hold.

To hold what is between man and woman, begin by emptying. By losing there is finding; by emptying there is filling. The shape that holds everything is emptiness.

As fish swim within water and birds fly within air, mind thinks within emptiness.

Forget everything. With not one thought to think and balance, let mind be shapeless and empty like sea allowing fish to float, like air allowing clouds to be.

Outside mind...just ordinary emptiness. Inside mind...just ordinary fullness.

158. All the Emptying Of River

The river flows into the sea but the sea never fills and the river never empties.

When all the flowing of water does not empty the river, how can there be emptiness? When all the emptying of river does not fill the sea, how much then can emptiness hold?

Within the river of words and the sea of thoughts, there is something that cannot be named. All thinking empties and fills around a still something.

For man and woman, in the flowing of each into other and the receiving of each by other, how much there is in the still knowing of filling and emptying.

As river fills into emptiness and sea receives into fullness, man and woman flow into each other, trusting endless emptying and filling.

Receiving is emptiness and fullness; filling is fullness and emptiness.

159. Empty Into Emptiness

Leaf, when it is being leaf, cannot understand tree. Fish when it is being fish, cannot understand sea. How can man, when he is being man, understand woman? And how can woman, when she is being woman, understand man?

Outside each thing is the emptiness that receives and fills and understands.

Be man but find not-man. Be woman but find not-woman. Soften. Trust the Tao. Let go of man and woman and empty into emptiness.

160. What Is and What Is Not

The fullness that is, is male; the emptiness that is not, is female. What is and what is not equally make wholeness.

His maleness is form, the full and visible, the shown and revealed. He is the spoken, the obvious and the apparent; the answer without the first question.

Her femaleness is formless, the empty and invisible, the hidden and concealed. She is the unspoken, the secret and the mystery; the first question without an answer.

161. Is and Is-Not

What is, is; what is not, also is.

The emptiness of man is outside, excluded, beyond and forgotten. The emptiness in woman is inside, included, within and remembered.

She is the reminder that both is and is-not are. He is the reminder that is-not is easily forgotten.

162. Fullness Carrying Emptiness

Woman shares with man the bones and flesh of body but she is also female. She is moving emptiness and moving waiting; an emptiness for man waiting to be filled.

She is garden and earth, mother and source, emptiness and mystery. She is woman, the moving and waiting riddle of is and is-not.

Within the great emptiness, woman is fullness carrying emptiness.

163. Fullness Desires

It is woman who receives filling and man who fills receiving. So emptiness is filled and refilled, and fullness is emptied and re-emptied.

Fullness desires to fill; emptiness desires to empty.

164. Because There Is Emptiness

Man and woman meet in emptiness, grow in emptiness, are filled in emptiness.

Because there is emptiness, there is receiving. Because there is receiving, there is giving. Because there is giving, there is fullness. Fullness arises out of emptiness. Fullness is the way to know emptiness.

To know the fullness of woman, be received by her emptiness. Shaped by emptiness, she is source and keeper of hidden knowing.

Emptiness cannot be found. Together as man and woman, use what cannot be found, fill what cannot be filled, and all the while come closer to emptiness.

165. Woman's Emptiness

Even the strongest muscle can be bent, the hardest stone broken. How invincible then is woman's emptiness. How can the male that is, overcome the female that is not? What can be greater than emptiness?

166. Always Waiting

When man is not ready, he cannot be lover; his fullness must be full. But woman's emptiness is always waiting.

167. Surrounding The Emptiness

Surrounding the emptiness that is female is the body that is woman. Woman defines the emptiness that is sought and filled by male.

Thinking only female, man remembers only emptiness and forgets woman. The sacred space requires also the honouring of the temple.

Beyond the thought of man and woman, is the thoughtlessness of man-woman. To be thoughtless, man may forget woman only when woman forgets man.

168. Body of Earth

The firmness of rock is known because of the compliance of water, the weight of earth because of the lightness of air. What is known when the fullness of man enters the emptiness of woman and her emptiness welcomes his fullness.

Body of earth and breath of air! Earth that is flesh of woman and bone of man! Air that is moving man and empty woman!

Where is the Tao if it is not here!

169. Accept the Breathing

When desire is spent, it arises again to be spent again. Like the breathing body, it is full to be emptied, filled to be emptied again.

How gracious that filling should be the beginning of emptying and emptying should be the beginning of filling; that the way of things is to use and be renewed.

Accept the breathing. Release this moment and receive the next...effortlessly.

While holding breath, the sky becomes brittle, the stars crack and the breathing earth grows hard.

170. Like the Breathing Tao

Lovers in union move with the rhythm of tides and seasons and generations. They fill and empty each other like the breathing Tao.

Filling empties and emptying fills. Each follows the other urging what is next.

Everything moves. Everything changes. Except the changing Tao.

171. In Such a Meeting

Man says, "Give me woman that with my body I may take her and fill her."

Woman says, "Give me man that with my body I may take him and enclose him."

Man, with all his fullness, fills the universe. Woman, with all her emptiness, encloses the universe.

What things must happen in such a meeting!

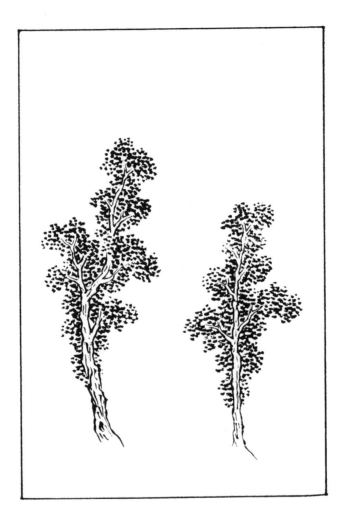

172. The Humility of Knowing

When man loses the strength of his fullness, he is unmade as man. When woman loses the lure of her emptiness, she is unmade as woman.

Man needs the humility of knowing he can be emptied; woman needs the humility of knowing she can be filled.

173. Only the Passing Stays

Woman is the universe of emptiness that man cannot fill. With brief pride, when woman is most filled, he is emptied of his fullness and returned to his beginning.

Man is the universe of fullness that woman cannot keep. With brief pride, when man is most taken, he empties of his fullness and she is returned to her beginning.

The wise know that in the rhythm of filling and emptying only the passing stays. Knowing this, they proceed with humility and thus balance. By letting go...they take hold of the Tao. By taking hold of the Tao...they let go.

174. The Lover's Balance

No skills, no powers are required. Only opening and trusting. The child returns as lover; bare and innocent and ready, afraid and eager.

When everything has been opened and released, when emptiness is full, there is the lovers' balance.

The Tao cannot be kept. Neither is it the keeper.

175. More Than Greatest

By giving, man fills woman and empties her of emptiness; by taking, woman receives man and empties him of fullness.

Where is fullness when it has been taken, and emptiness when it has been filled?

The filling of one and the emptying of other fills the emptiness that was in both.

When man empties into the filled emptiness of woman, it is more than his greatest giving. And when woman takes of his emptying fullness, it is more than her greatest taking.

What is more than greatest? What can be named that is greater than greatest?

176. The Tao's Breath

The mystery is man entering woman and woman receiving man. The mystery is outside fullness finding inside emptiness and inside emptiness knowing outside fullness. The mystery of man and woman is the union of fullness and emptiness so there is no longer fullness or emptiness. The mystery is fullness emptying into filled emptiness to be taken by woman and grown into her fullness that she may empty.

Filling and emptying! Breathing the seasons and generations! Everything is the Tao's breath.

What is it that breathes? No one can say. But every motion is a breath in the everywhere of that breathing.

177. Forbidden Yet Promised

They are strange yet common, odd yet honoured, cautioning yet enticing, forbidden yet promised.

Dare man enter? Dare woman take?

178. In an Endless Beginning

Out of man's rising and his emptying into woman comes his own falling and her rising fullness. Out of woman's fullness and her emptying comes the world's filling by birth and its emptying by death. Filling comes from emptying; emptying comes from filling. It is as if, in an endless beginning, nothing is lost or gained.

Woman is the honoured and dishonoured breathing rhythm of taking and giving. Man is her accomplice in breath, implicated by the urge in his own breathing.

179. Waiting Emptiness

When man is not filling woman with his fullness, there is always for him her waiting emptiness. Though filled and filled again, she remains unfilled and waiting. Fullness cannot overcome great waiting emptiness.

When woman is not taking man and emptying him with her emptiness, there is always for her his rising fullness. Though emptied and emptied again, he returns full and waiting. Emptiness cannot overcome great rising fullness.

180. Its Own Other Body

Union is the coming home of one body to its own other body. As man and woman, be together in complete ease.

Man is fullness and woman is his emptiness. With only body thinking, he reaches in for his emptiness and receives himself.

Woman is emptiness and man is her fullness. With only body thinking, she reaches out for her fullness and fills herself.

Union

181. So Much Is Found

There is and there is also is-not. Male is is, seeking is-not; female is is-not, seeking is. So it is that in union so much is found.

182. Without Question

Rather than man taking woman or woman taking man, it is better when they are taken by each other. When desire arises out of each other, there is no beginning, no question and answer, no uncertainty.

Books cannot teach it. Words give the wrong answer. Think and it is already too late. Ask and the answer is no.

Water thoughtlessly finds its path. Seasons mindlessly fulfill the year.

Come together as waters meet, as seasons arrive. Without searching...be found.

Without question...the answer is yes.

183. From Moment To Moment

What is called the beginning requires as much attention as what is called the end. When bodies meet, unless taken by hurry, do not hurry.

Each moment is a beginning, each moment an ending. From moment to moment there is nothing else to do, nowhere else to go, nothing else to be.

184. With the Readiness of Knowing

As man, enter and move with the readiness of knowing and the freshness of not knowing.

As woman, take and move with the readiness of knowing and the freshness of not knowing.

Thus the new does not overcome and the old is renewed.

185. Please the Primal Play

Alone together, there is no need for restraint. Walls and curtains, warmth and moon draw lovers into each other to inhale more than their ordinary selves.

Please the primal play of bodies dancing their own breathing in the Great Mother's magic.

186. All the Ancient Steps

What has not yet been done together and wants to be done...do. Gently and fully empty and open and flow into the mysteries of each other.

Countless others have come together practicing the extraordinary ordinary. All our ancestors have been preparing us for now.

With both bodies, dance all the ancient steps.

187. Only Body Knows

When man's fullness has been taken by woman, he is no longer mysterious man; when woman's emptiness has been filled with man, she is no longer mysterious woman. Together as man-woman, woman-man, there is another mystery.

Hold to separate man and woman and union will not be understood.

Union is something...something more than words' illusions can say. Like shadows, words follow thoughts, thoughts follow mind, mind follows body. How can union be understood when only body knows?

When words fail, the Tao is somewhere near.

188. Bodies Understand the Tao

Union is not just outside entering inside and inside receiving outside; it is the act of man and woman reconciling each other with themselves.

Bodies understand the Tao. They unite their separates, resolve their opposites. Two bodies as one are like the one of the Tao.

189. Beyond Union

For man, his greatness fills the universe until there is only hardness...seeking. This is the greatness of man.

How gracious that there should be a place where such greatness is held and encompassed. This is the greatness of woman within whom man tries.

Beyond man's trying and woman's holding, there is something else. Beyond union there is something that is...more than filling the universe, more than encompassing the universe. Words point but will not say.

What is before thought and birth, before urge knows itself? What is full emptiness and empty fullness? Where are there no questions and happening is just itself?

190. Undoing Different

Winter and summer reconcile themselves. East and west come to each other. Manifest in year and earth is the wholeness of man and woman.

Call their four arms the four seasons, their four legs the four directions. Limbs and bodies enwrap toward oneness, entwining and holding. Twos weave by twos, and one finds one. The special encloses the special, undoing different and separate.

191. Deep Within Living Everything

From somewhere deep within living everything, there is something beyond thought and knowing. It could be called nothing, yet from it comes arising, then urge, then desire, then passion.

When fullness and emptiness unite and passion empties both man and woman to wholeness, they are returned to a new arising of something deep within their living.

192. Lovers Find What Sages Seek

Together in passion, man and woman go beyond each other to the moving stillness beyond self. Opposites resolve. Man and woman are no more. In the thoughtless primal that is the Tao, one and two are none and all.

Lovers find what sages seek. Body and mind disappear. Division and separation end. And the being that is all, overcomes the thinking that is some.

Those who touch all do not return to some the same.

193. Passing and Becoming

Air and fire arise from water and earth. The hot outside breath kindles the hot inside breath.

Each lover arises out of the other and disappears into both.

Earth stirs earth and arouses breath and flesh. Fire ignites fire.

The pushing of earth against earth urges the waters of both into the wet and spume of passing and becoming.

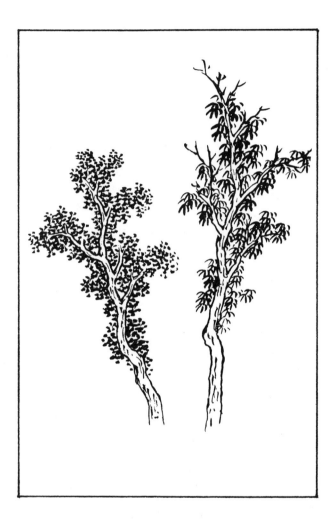

194. Earth Breathes Itself

In moving union, man and woman inhale and exhale each other like body breathing body.

Earth breathes itself in lovers. Each is the other's air of earth that charges with breath the water and fire of flesh.

In breathing together as lovers, breathe in and out each other in service of each and both and all.

Hold breaths...and the whole earth waits.

195. The Need of Each

Fulfillment in man arises from his pleasing of woman. Fulfillment in woman arises from her pleasing of man.

The pleasing of each by other strengthens each and both together.

The need of each is the feeding of other and both.

196. Full Range

In love making, permit each other full range.

If it cannot be gotten from each other, where can it be gotten?

Each body is the other's feast. As host...offer fully. As guest...take respectfully.

197. Taking the River's Time

The river flows of itself. Uninstructed...it finds its way to the sea.

The downward way of wisdom takes all toward union in deep fullness.

Flow easily downward, without hurry, taking the river's time.

Know that the urge in blood and all its rushing is toward the great commingling pool.

Remember downward and trust the river's way.

198. A Beginning Of the Beginning

If there must be a beginning then there must be a beginning of the beginning. Then there must be a beginning of the beginning of the beginning. How then can any beginning be the beginning?

In every beginning there is desire and from desire arises every beginning. The universe is desire, arising from itself and fulfilling itself, just as moving water is the river.

When man and woman unite, every star and blade of grass moves in accord with them. There cannot be error when desire's roots are in the stars and its urge is also in the grasses.

Man and woman come together enacting the one of everything, then they separate enacting the parts of everything. Subsiding desire separates; separation arouses desire; aroused desire unites. The rhythm of days and seasons is the rhythm of lovers and generations.

Desire was there with the Tao even before the beginning of every beginning.

199. Mere Body

The way beyond limits is within limits. The way out is in. So it is with everything.

As mind knows the way beyond mind, body knows the way beyond body. From body's centre need of ache and urge arises the leap of body beyond body.

Who can tell self from other, inner from outer, thinking from doing when mind is not thinking, when touching is thinking only touching, and body is thoughtlessly dancing body. And then...not even body.

Surrender to know. Lose to find. Mere body is quite enough.

200. Mind Follows Body's Thinking

Body already knows what to do. Mind follows body's thinking, inventing thoughts to understand what is already known.

Then amazed mind watches desire arise and, entranced by body's thinking, forgets everything until the moving and lifting overcomes and mind is flooded with insight.

201. Let Body Decide

Moving releases the releasing. Hold tight and it will not let go. Urge and it will not come. It is within and so close yet it cannot be grasped. Let body decide for itself.

When releasing comes and takes and overcomes, it comes of itself from a deep and waiting readiness where earth tricks itself joyfully to lure us over and over again from day to day. It comes from the within that we are within, from something that becomes but does not begin. Though us, it is not ours. It teaches us how to go in this world, not as mover, but as moving.

202. Eyes Distant and Fresh

Beyond moving union is the still place, the great waiting that summons but will not itself come. So man and woman move toward it, moving the world to stopping, collapsing the stillness to moving.

This easy struggle shudders earth and brings to an end with new beginning the same old world. With eyes distant and fresh, lovers return to another beginning that each time renews the familiar with grace.

203. Its Own Returning Time

Like the seasons, desire waits, stirs, excites and then fulfills.

The rhythm of the year is the promise that releases lovers to autumn's ending. Their moving autumn union is the rhythm of new beginnings. Deep in their summer blood they know the unspoken promise and so let go.

Even the common quiet of winter's waiting is the keeping of that promise. And even winter's thoughtfulness trusts that desire will find its own returning time.

204. By Body's Doing

When man's fullness has been taken by woman's emptiness and woman's emptiness has been filled by man's fullness, there is no longer just man and woman. They are transformed and harmonized by body's doing.

This is man-mind and woman-mind understanding so easily with flesh what thinking cannot do with thoughts.

See how thoughts chase after body trying to understand with thinking what bodies know so easily with flesh.

205. The Simple and Obvious

In the obvious there is something not obvious. In the simple there is something not simple. The simple and obvious are not simple and obvious.

When man and woman meet in deep touching, there is something more than body meeting body. Within the between of them, there is something that joins inner with outer, here with there, this with that.

Within the between of them there is something ordinary and extraordinary: a moving stillness; a full emptiness; a becoming that is neither thought nor thing, that touches without touching. Thoughts cannot find it because of mind; senses cannot feel it because of body.

When body meets body in deep touching, take hold of the becoming that is between. With mind thinking between thoughts, and body feeling between bodies, it is so obvious, so simple.

The union of man and woman just teaches that the becoming between them is between everything.

206. Both Feet Must Dance

When woman's emptiness has been filled and man's fullness has been emptied, each has unmade the other.

Man will have his fall and his need for woman's holding of his great fullness is his blame of her for his unmaking. Man falls to newness through emptying by the woman-mother.

Woman will have her fall and her need for man's filling of her great emptiness is her blame of him for her unmaking. Woman falls to newness through filling by the man-father.

Every losing is a finding of new balance. The falling greatness of man and woman to each other is the losing of separateness to find togetherness. Their bodies have always known the whole balance of union but their minds' definitions must be convinced by their bodies' persuasion. It is the closeness of touching that undoes the distance of thinking. Close bodies show thinking minds how to understand.

All union reminds minds' forgetfulness that bodies will have their way.

Full balance is equal mind and body, equal man and woman. To realize the Tao, both feet must dance.

207. A Special Stillness

In the space between each thought and act is a special stillness that carries from stillness to stillness giving balance to thought and act.

Everything arises from and returns to stillness. Stillness is the ease in which non-thinking and non-doing happen of themselves.

Even in union is stillness...so no effort at all; just bodies non-doing their bodies and minds in stillness playing awareness.

208. The Effortless Effort

Within the moving union of man and woman is the stillness of inside meeting outside, of one meeting other, of incompletes completing.

As body moves itself, keep the stillness where mind plays being mind while body plays being body.

Union is the resting place of man and woman, the effortless effort, the still and quiet rushing silence.

209. Without Man and Woman

In that motionless moment of union when woman has taken all of man and is full, nothing more can be taken when all her emptiness has been filled. And when all of man has been given to her emptiness, nothing more can be given when all his fullness has been taken. Man unmakes woman and woman unmakes man.

Man's giving all and woman's taking all is the losing of both, the emptying of two into the one that is neither.

Is this really so? Without man and woman, who will answer yes or no?

210. Amazing Now

Lovers in union are without person when he is beyond self and does not know himself and when she is beyond self and does not know herself.

When to him she is beyond object and is no longer thing, he does not know her. When to her he is beyond object and is no longer thing, she does not know him.

Not possessing desire, they are desire. Joined together, they are the dream of this most amazing now.

211. Each Time's Return

Before their end and their beginning again, they are two embracing lovers held in mindless wonder. Where is their separateness? Where is their differentness? Where are the two that are one?

Single bodyness dizzies thought until there is release, and end, and mind again, and then beginning that settles into separation and a new time for once more the primal awakening.

What could be wiser in the nature of things than each time's return to the arousing beginning?

212. The Other Half Of Wholeness

In union, when man gives to woman and woman gives to man, each gives to other the other half of wholeness.

More than each are both, fulfilling the urge for togetherness. More than both are each, fulfilling the urge for separateness.

Biography

Ray Grigg lives with his wife in a house they built together in a forested area on Quadra Island, in British Columbia, Canada.

He received his two bachelor's degrees in English/Psychology and in Education from the University of British Columbia, where he also studied fine arts and philosophy. "The psychology and philosophy convinced me that the subjective cannot be objectified; the English and fine arts convinced me that the mystery is deeper than can be explained." It was during this time that he became interested in Zen and Taoism, "because they somehow felt whole and balanced, somehow connecting my head with my feet."

From 1965 to 1987 he taught in several senior secondary schools of British Columbia, teaching English, English literary history, fine arts, and cultural history. In addition he designed and taught a course on world religions that included studies in Judaism, Christianity, Islam, Hinduism, Buddhism, Taoism and Zen.

Before and between teaching assignments, he traveled extensively in no fewer than forty countries, and considers this to be a major shaping force in his vision of life.

He is currently devoting himself full time to writing. "The writing I am doing feels to me like it has a certain sense of 'completion.' I think, I do; and yet there is really nothing to think, nothing to do. The intellectual struggles, the travel with words accomplishes nothing and leads nowhere. But the journey must be made because it is the only way the beginning can be found. All my words are about finding the beginning. This is why the essence of Zen and Taoism are so important—because they always point us back to the beginning so we can carry on wisely after arriving."

Books about Taoism and Related Matters

Brand, Stuart, ed. The Next Whole Earth Catalog. New York: Point Random House, 1980.

Bynner, Witter. The Way of Life According to Laotzu. New York: Capricorn Books, 1962.

Capra, Fritjof. The Tao of Physics. Berkeley, CA: Shambala, 1975.

Feng, Gai-fu, and Jane English. Tao Te Ching. New York: Alfred A. Knopf, 1972.

Heider, John. The Tao of Leadership. Atlanta: Humanics New Age, 1985.

Medhurst, Spurgeon. The Tao-Teh-King. Wheaton, IL: The Theosophical Publishing House, 1972.

Schmidt, K.O. Tao Te Ching (Lao-Tse's Book of Life). Lakemont, GA: CSA Press, 1975.

Schwenk, Theodore. Sensitive Chaos. New York: Schocken Books, 1965.

Vanden Broek, Goldian, ed. Less is More; The Art of Voluntary Poverty. Harper Colophon Books. New York: Harper & Row, 1978.

Waley, Arthur. The Way and Its Power. New York: Grove Press, 1958.

Watts, Alan, and Al Chung-liang Huang. Tao the Watercourse Way. New York: Pantheon Books, 1975.

Wilhelm, Richard, and Cary Baynes, trans. I Ching or The Book of Changes. Princeton, NJ: Princeton University Press, 1967.

Other New Books From Humanics New Age

For Couples Only
Billie S. Ables, Ph.D.

Most couples fight, but most don't really know why they do. Every relationship has hidden "rules" unconsciously established by the partners. Until these rules are understood the conflicts will continue. Dr. Ables shows how couples tend to act with their partners as they did with their parents. **For Couples Only** gives straightforward strategies for enhancing awareness of you and your mate.

Life Trek: The Odyssey of Adult Development
John Stockmyer, M.S. and Robert Williams, Ph.D.

Life Trek is a chronological journey for the reader through the stages and patterns of adult life from 18-80–and beyond. Based on the latest research, and original contributions by the authors, the book blends historical fables with traditional psychology to point out the timeless nature of the many challenges that affect people throughout each decade of life. Two innovative simulation games are included, giving the reader the exciting opportunity to "play out" his or her own life. The **Life Trek** games even permit the reader to play the life of someone completely different.

Body, Self, and Soul: Sustaining Integration
Jack Lee Rosenberg, D.D.S., Ph.D., Marjorie L. Rand, Ph.D., and Diane Assay, M.A.

An introduction to an exciting new therapy method developed by the author of the best seller *TOTAL ORGASM* and his associates. This therapy, called Integrative Body Psychotherapy, blends ideas from East and West, including Tantric and Hatha yoga; Freudian, Jungian, Reichian, and Gestalt therapies; Rolfing and meditation. Fascinating case studies show how this comprehensive approach can result in profound, lasting changes.

These books and other Humanics New Age publications are available from booksellers or from Humanics New Age, P.O. Box 7447, Atlanta, Georgia, 30309, 1-800-874-8844. Call or write for your free copy of our publications brochure.